MYSTIC MICHIGAN
Part One
I

By Mark Jager

Revised
Fifth Edition

MYSTIC MICHIGAN
PART ONE
Revised
By Mark Jager

Published by
ZOSMA PUBLICATIONS
PO Box 24
Hersey, Michigan 49639

Copyright 2007 by Mark A. Jager
Fifth Edition Revised Volume One 2007

ISBN 0-9672464-4-X

Cover Photo
by Deana Jager
Copyright 2006

God stretched forth
His mystic hand
and wrote great wonders
upon the sea and land.

Contents

Ancient Statues

Ancient statues and a tablet inscribed with hieroglyphics were unearthed in Newberry in 1896. A man named John McGruer owned a 40-acre parcel of land near Newberry.

One day he sent some workers out on his property to chop wood. When they saw a mink run into a hole underneath a hemlock tree, they began digging for it. They proceeded to unearth three statues and an ancient tablet etched with mysterious hieroglyphics. The statues were of a man, woman and a child. They were made of clay, and were badly damaged by the workers digging them out. These Newberry statues are on display at the Dubuade Museum in St. Ignace.

The tablet was sent to Dr. Barry Fell, a professor at Harvard University. Fell concluded that the writing on the tablet was in Cypriot-Minoan and from the island of Cypress. The hieroglyphic can be read across or down because it was written in a puzzle-like style.

According to the book *Superior Heartland, by Fred Rydholm*, Cypress is where copper was first mined. It seems logical for the Cypriots to come to Michigan for the copper deposits. The Keweenaw Peninsula is the largest source of pure copper in the world. Some believe that Michigan copper was used to build the Great Pyramid.

Bigfoot

Art Kapa, of Mayville, is Michigan's unofficial Bigfoot expert. Kapa has investigated approximately 225 reported sightings of the hairy creature in Michigan since 1968. He believes more people have seen Bigfoot but do not report it.

In 1964, a berry picker reported seeing a nine-foot-tall creature in the Sister Lakes area. In 1976, near Camp Grayling, reports state that a Bigfoot chased three military men into their truck. Several years ago, Art investigated a sighting near the Au Sable River. People hiking near the river saw movement in a pine grove and heard a horrendous scream. Then a creature ran across the river and into the wilderness.

Kapa claims he has casts of the footprints of Bigfoot. The largest cast, obtained from Hillsdale County, is almost twenty-three inches long. The steps were about forty-two inches apart. The average human step is about twenty-eight inches apart.

Art has tape recordings of a strange animal screaming, unlike anything he had ever heard, that he believes could be Bigfoot. He also has a hair sample, found by researchers, that he believes came from a Bigfoot.

The elusive "Michigander" known as Bigfoot continues to mystify many in the forests of Michigan.

Bottomless Lakes

There are a significant number of lakes and ponds scattered throughout Michigan with the ominous reputation of being "bottomless". Of these so-called bottomless lakes and ponds, there seem to be two types.

The first is fed by an underground stream. One such lake is Higgins Lake in North-Central Michigan. Because of certain fish found in the lake, some believe it is fed by an underground stream that connects to Lake Huron. Higgins Lake is one of the deepest inland lakes in Michigan and those who fish it are best off having an extremely long anchor line.

The second type of bottomless lake or pond is one with a murky bottom that serves like a type of quicksand. There are farmers who claim they have lost horses and cattle in these murky death traps. In such cases, even after raking the bottom of the lake, there was no sign of the creature anywhere.

Historically, people who had these murky, bottomless ponds on their property would take advantage of them by using them to discard refuse. If it were possible to examine the murky ground beneath these lakes and ponds, perhaps many antique treasures could be recovered.

Caves

Many people are surprised to discover that Michigan has a number of caves and caverns to explore. The Michigan Karst Conservancy owns two preserves that are open to the public. The 480-acre Fiborn Karst Preserve, in the Upper Peninsula, features caves, sinkholes and disappearing streams.

The only show cave in the Great Lakes area is in Buchanan, Michigan. "Bear Cave" is formed in rare "tufa rock" (a secondary limestone). Geologists estimate the cave to be at least 25,000 years old. Visitors enter the cave through a gift shop and exit through a second entrance near a waterfall. Striking stalactites and flowstone can be viewed throughout the cave.

In 1875, the loot from a bank robbery in Ohio was hidden in Bear Cave. The 1903 movie *The Great Train Robbery* was inspired by this incident and Bear Cave is actually featured in the film.

One of the most recently discovered caves in Michigan is the Portage Bay cave, in Delta County. The Michigan Karst Conservancy mapped the cave in August 1993.

There are also many sea caves and caverns in the Great Lakes. Michigan's biggest known cave is the Hendrie water cave.

The Curious Canal

Many over the decades have considered the canal in Cadillac that connects Lake Mitchell and Lake Cadillac an enigma. This is because the canal exhibits an unusual water phenomenon. Even Ripley's Believe-It-Or-Not has mentioned this peculiar occurrence.

Ever since the construction of the canal, in the late 1800's, people wonder why the canal freezes over when the cold weather comes, while the lakes remain unfrozen. Later, when the lakes freeze over, the canal thaws out and remains unfrozen for the rest of the winter.

Although the canal's behavior is unusual, the DNR says there is an explanation. The water in the canal is the shallowest, and that is why it freezes first. Once the lakes freeze, the weight of the ice pushing down forces the warmer water from the bottom of the lake, up and through the canal. There is also a natural flow of water going from Lake Mitchell to Lake Cadillac, on its way to the Clam River at the other end of Lake Cadillac. These two conditions melt the ice in the canal.

Edward Meyer (*Vice President of exhibits and archives, Ripley's Believe-It-Or-Not*) says that after receiving updated information and proof of the phenomenon, they will include it in Ripley's Believe-It-Or-Not syndicated cartoon form.

Dolmen Altars

On top of the rocky Huron Mountain in Michigan's Upper Peninsula is a strange rock formation that some believe to be an ancient Norse altar. John Longyear of the Arctic Coal Company first discovered the stone configuration in 1873.

The formation consists of three large rocks, set in a triangular form, with a large boulder perched on top. Some theorize that the "altar" was used for religious ceremonies by travelers who came to mine copper on the Keweenaw Peninsula. Some believed the mysterious rock structures called "dolmens" were placed in magical locations.

Various researchers believe that Vikings, who traveled on the Great Lakes before Columbus, built it.

Floating Island

There are many interesting islands in Michigan; however, one of them takes the prize for being the strangest. Lake Dubonnet, near Interlochen, is the home of a one-acre island covered with forty-foot trees and underbrush that floats back and forth across the surface of the lake wherever the wind happens to blow it. Even though its movements are slow, anglers report that at times they have returned to their favorite fishing spot, only to discover the island covering it.

Officials from the DNR have witnessed the island slowly moving across the lake while setting up nets for a fishing survey. Since the island is so slow to move, one's chances of seeing it actually move are slim. However, if weather conditions are right, the island can be seen drifting.

The floating island on Lake Dubonnet is not the only one in Michigan; it is just one of the best known. There have been reports from a number of different campers and anglers of these types of islands in several inland lakes in Michigan.

Ghost Fire

For centuries, brilliant exhibitions of the Northern Lights have amazed Michiganders. The flaming whirlpools of light swirl around in a mystical and unpredictable way. The scientific name of the Northern Lights is Aurora Borealis. They are also known as lost lightning, airglow, fire of the Arctic Ocean and ghost fire.

The Eskimos believed that the Northern Lights were sacred flames lit by angel-like spirits to guide and illuminate celestial travelers on their way to heaven. They believed that the lights were living and that if you whistled at them they would draw near to you.

The Salteaux Indians of Eastern Canada interpreted the lights as dancing spirits. In other superstitions, they are the spirits of departed children playing and dancing in the starry night sky. Because of the latitude of Italy and France, the Northern Lights are a reddish color. Years ago, people there viewed them as an evil omen that signified death.

The Aurora Borealis appear throughout the year in Michigan and chances of seeing them are good. The orchestrated light shows of the night are an awesome part of the magic of the north.

Gravity Hill

It is estimated by those who live in the vicinity of *Gravity Hill* in Benzie County, that between one and two thousand people come to experience the effects of what may be a vortex in the Earth's magnetic field.

Objects placed at the bottom of a hill, along a quarter-mile section of Putney Road in Blaine Township, will roll *uphill* in excess of fifteen miles per-hour. The area that seems to defy gravity is only miles from the forty-fifth parallel; the latitude that marks the halfway point between the equator and the North Pole. Whether the spot is a magnetic freak of nature or an optical illusion is a matter of speculation. Whatever the explanation, some view the area as a special place.

Perhaps the immediate surroundings of Gravity Hill have made it more mysterious. At the top of the hill rests the remains of a ghost town and a church, that is over one-hundred years old.

Cars placed in neutral will roll up the hill to the parking lot of the old church. Legends have persisted that the church is trying to pull people back to it. Is it possible that some of the settlers who came and built the church at the top of the hill viewed the area as a supernatural place?

Map of Gravity Hill
in Blaine Township

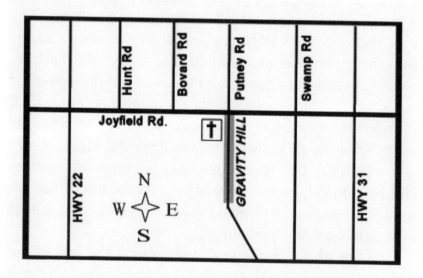

Great Lakes Triangle

The Great Lakes have gained a reputation for being mysterious and unpredictable; there are forces at work that command respect. An estimated three to eight thousand ships have sunk in the Great Lakes, more than in the Bermuda Triangle.

A number of ships worth countless historical and monetary value lay beneath the veiling waters of the Great Lakes. One of the French explorer La Salle's ships, the "Griffen", was one of the first ships to be lost. A treasure ship that sunk during the Civil War was carrying gold coins worth an estimated ten to twenty-five million dollars by today's standards.

A number of planes have also disappeared almost instantly in the Great Lakes. Many accidents are due to adverse weather conditions like unrelenting fog or winter's blinding snowstorms. However, ships and planes have vanished from radar just as instantly during calm seas. Some ships have been lost in broad daylight.

There are a number of shipwreck museums in Michigan, preserving the reverential awe of the Great Lakes. Nine underwater preserves are located throughout the Great Lakes, offering a high concentration of shipwrecks for divers to explore. In Petoskey, an underwater marble pathway beneath the waters of Lake Michigan, leads divers to a large crucifix.

Green Sunsets

Occasionally, just as the sun appears to sink into the crystal blue waters of the Great Lakes, a small, still visible part of the sun will turn a bright and illuminating green. This phenomenon happens so fast it is referred to as the "green flash". Similarly, a fleeting ray or glow of green, that shoots up from the sunset is known as a "green ray".

The green flash is related to mirages that, as mentioned previously in this book, the Great Lakes produce. The rare spectacle is caused, in part, by atmospheric refraction. There is a point just before the sun goes down that all the hues of the color spectrum are blocked out, except green.

Although many folks are unaware that such a spectacle exists, some native Michiganders have enjoyed this marvel for years. There is a group in Empire called "The Green Flash Society" who seeks to heighten public awareness and enjoy venturing out to watch for this rare exhibition.

Many clear Michigan nights contribute to viewing this incredible evening sky-show. Stand at a point higher than the horizon. It helps to use an optical aid like binoculars or field glasses. Keep watching, even after the Sun has disappeared; the Sun might reappear, owing to waves on the water or in the air, and give a "green flash".

Historical Indian Highways

There is an ancient highway in northwestern Lower Michigan. Those who travel its fading lanes often find themselves on a journey that leads them back in time. Faded and worn stone markers remain at certain sections of the Cadillac to Traverse City Indian trail, pointing the way, down an old highway that was nearly lost in the pages of time.

Some of the things discovered along the trail are Native American campsites, fire-pits, burial mounds and artifacts. A silver cross, believed to have belonged to a Jesuit priest, was unearthed along the trail near Buckley. The French explorer La Salle, known to have visited Michigan at one time, is the presumed owner of a sword and armor discovered along the trail.

There was a science to the trail construction. Places along the trail have wagon wheel imprints that give witness to the fact that the trail later became a roadway for stagecoaches. Evidence indicates that the trail was not a haphazard undertaking, but was part of an elaborate statewide highway system. The paths followed the areas of least resistance and crossed rivers where they were the shallowest. Records indicate that because of the systematical planning of the trails, they later became modern highways. Mackinaw Trail in Cadillac and parts of U.S. 131 are examples.

Largest Living Organism

It may sound like something from a science fiction movie, but one of the largest forms of life known to exist is growing in a forest in the Upper Peninsula.

In the early 1990's researchers from Michigan Tech and the University of Toronto discovered a giant fungus known as an *armillaria bulbosa* or "honey mushroom". Upon its discovery, researchers estimated that the fungus was at least 1,500 years old and one of the largest and oldest living things on Earth.

The interweaving mushrooms and tentacles growing near Crystal Falls, Michigan, cover an area of thirty-eight acres. The fungus is estimated to grow at a rate of eight inches a year.

Spawned by a single spore, it is a thriving, solitary organism, well suited to its environment. The massive fungus feeds on dead tree roots and grows underground. Individual mushrooms that shoot to the surface each fall is the only visible part of the organism.

The giant fungus received national attention when it was first discovered and was labeled the world's largest living thing. Since the discovery of this "honey mushroom", other larger ones have been discovered.

The town of Crystal Falls dubbed the unique discovery the "humungus fungus" and hosts the "Humungus Fungus Festival" each August in its honor.

The Legend of Lake Superior

The magnificent Lake Superior is the world's largest freshwater lake, or rather "inland sea". The surface area spans 31,700 square miles, and plunges to depths of over 1,300 feet. Among other things, it could swallow the other four Great Lakes plus three more bodies of water the size of Lake Erie.

The Indians had a reverent understanding of how quickly this giant lake could unleash the enormous supremacy of 2,900 cubic miles of water. They usually offered a sacrifice before traveling on the Great Lakes.

A legend lives on from the Chippewa Indians that states Lake Superior fails to give up its dead. The Indians may have thought the manitous, that they believe governed the lakes, took the un-recovered bodies. The most famous tale concerning this phenomenon is the wreck of the Edmond Fitzgerald. The boat sunk during a storm, the evening of November 10, 1975. Researchers have speculated that the answer to the absence of recovered corpses may lie in the underwater caverns at the bottom of Lake Superior. If explorers searched the caves in the deep, dark waters of Superior, is it possible that they would find numerous corpses? The icy condition of Lake Superior is renowned and another explanation is that the waters are so cold that it thwarts the dead from decomposing or floating to the surface.

The Lost Geometrical Gardens

Archaeologist found ancient gardens in the early 1900's. At least twenty-three unique, geometrically designed plots are in Michigan. Some of these garden beds were situated in an area between the southwestern corner of Berrien County and the head of Saginaw Bay. Others were located for miles along the St. Joseph and Grand Rivers, where they grew in the fertile prairie-land.

A garden near the Kalamazoo area resembled a large wagon wheel. The circular plot was ninety-feet in circumference, with rows extending, like spokes, out from an inner circle, to an elevated outer ridge.

There were much larger configurations found in other parts of the state. In some places, there were rectangular garden beds, over one-hundred acres in size. The designs appeared much older than the designs of the Algonquian Indian tribes that resided in Michigan. These types of gardens have existed throughout history in other parts of the world, such as in the ancient kingdom of Babylon.

Although time and modern civilization have erased these ancient garden beds, very good diagrams and measurements are preserved for record. For more information, or to recreate your own small-scale, "ancient geometrical garden" refer to *"Michigan Pioneer and Historical collections"*, volumes 2 and 14.

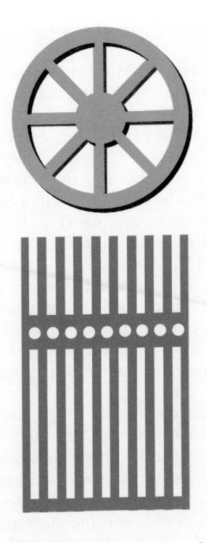

Ancient Geometrical Gardens

Meteorites

The University of Michigan discovered that two gigantic meteors struck Michigan thousands of years ago. The largest of the two meteor craters was discovered under the waters of Lake Huron, near Port Huron.

The circular crater is located more than a mile underneath the bed of Lake Huron and is thirty miles in diameter. It is anywhere from a half-mile to a mile deep. The crater is the largest ever found in the United States and is the third or fourth biggest crater in the world, according to U of M astronomers.

The second crater lies just south of the small village of Calvin Center, and is buried about one to four-hundred feet beneath the surface. The meteor estimated to be about the size of a football stadium, hollowed out a crater five-miles across. Farm and forestlands cover the area now.

In 1895, a farmer named Ernest Ruppert found a forty-four pound meteorite in Reed City. A Reed City Hotel put the meteorite on display. In 1921, residents of Rose City saw a meteor fall and heard loud explosions when it landed. Two meteorites were discovered; one weighed thirteen pounds and the other weighed seven pounds. In 1994, a large meteorite crashed into Lake Michigan. TV broadcasters reported the event, and witnesses heard a loud explosion when it crashed.

Michigan's Place
On the Continent of Pangaea

Michigan may have held a very important position in the ancient world. Some researchers believe that in the past there was a super continent called Pangaea. If one examines the landmasses on both sides of the Atlantic Ocean, one may notice that it appears as if the continents fit together like a giant puzzle at one time.

Some geographers believe that before the continents split, Spain and New York probably touched at about the equator. They estimate that Michigan was about ten degrees north of the equator, near the north-central portion of the continent of Pangaea.

Because of its central position on the continent, some researchers believe that it may also have been a social center. Perhaps the inhabitants of the ancient continent of Pangaea built some of the ancient ruins in Michigan, such as the mini-Stonehenge located on Beaver Island.

Michigan's Stonehenge

A mysterious ancient circle of stones, similar to Stonehenge in England, was discovered in the underbrush, several years ago on Beaver Island. Its finding has led many archeologists and historians to believe that an unknown culture existed in Michigan that predated the Indians.

The Michigan "Stonehenge" is on private property. Because of increasing vandalism, historical authorities on the island prefer to keep the megalithic monument as a curiosity rather than a major tourist attraction.

The circular structure, made up of 39 stones, is 397 feet in diameter. The rocks vary in size, with the largest being ten feet thick. In the center of the configuration is a boulder, four feet high and five feet across, with a hole in the center that may have once held a pole.

There are many theories as to who built this mini-Stonehenge. Some say the Vikings, Phoenicians or Egyptian explorers. Others believe the Native Americans constructed it as a primitive calendar to track the movement of the sun. The center rod would have been used to distinguish the seasonal equinox and determine the growing seasons. Other Native Americans believe the circle may have a more spiritual significance.

Missaukee Mounds

Thousands of years before the Algonquian tribes arrived in Michigan; prehistoric people lived here who constructed peculiar mounds. These mounds of earth form large circular and serpentine shapes. The formations are still there today. Three circular ruins are in Missaukee County, and a horseshoe pattern exists in Wexford County. The larger of two formations found in Missaukee County is 190 feet in diameter. Its average elevation is five feet. The second structure, located a half-mile from the first, is 165 feet in diameter.

The structures, originally thought to be Indian burial mounds, contained no evidence that they were ever used for that purpose. Other theories state that they were constructed for lodging, forts, temples, dance circles, or ancient calendars.

The mounds are much older than had been previously thought. They were built hundreds of years before any of the Algonquian Indians arrived in the area.

The formations look like the circular structures the Philosopher Plato describes in his book about the lost continent of Atlantis. Some believe people who escaped from the lost continent of Atlantis built them. Others theorize the Addenda or Hopewell Indians, Egyptians, one of the lost tribes of the Israelites, or a pre-flood civilization, constructed them.

Mysterious Mirages

Michigan is a land of mirages and optical illusions, where what appears to be real, sometimes is not. Michigan is a mystical place where one's eye cannot always be trusted. The reason for the mystery is all around us: the Great Lakes.

Certain repeating weather patterns over the big lakes often contribute to mirages. A weather phenomenon known as "Arctic mirage" or cold air lensing, is common over large bodies of water or fields of ice. That means, of course, that it is common here too.

The images of light can travel hundreds of miles and give the viewer the ability to see over the edge of the horizon. From the shoreline of Michigan, people report seeing traffic, harbor lights and planes landing on the shoreline of Wisconsin. These images are visible over a distance of fifty to seventy miles. While Michigan mirages appear illusory, they are real, and can be photographed with cameras.

Around November, the lakes can get choppy, producing big vertical waves. When the weather conditions are right, the waves are magnified and appear bigger than they are. Sailors on the Great Lakes have seen optical illusions that involve the distortion of size and shape, some resembling Christmas trees.

The Paulding Lights

At one time, Ripley's Believe-It-Or-Not offered in excess in $1,000,000.00 to anyone who could solve a bizarre light spectacle in Paulding Michigan.

Nearly every clear evening, strange circular spheres of light dance on the horizon of the tiny community. At one point, they seem to follow a pathway of electrical lines. The roving lights have appeared as red, white and green. Do not confuse these odd luminaries with the Northern Lights; they are a phenomenon that is unique to Paulding, Michigan.

The TV program *Michigan Magazine* and *Marquette's Channel Six News* have captured the spectacle on film. The Michigan Forest Service has put up a sign, telling the legend of the Paulding lights and marks the spot to best view them. The legend reads:

"Legend explains its presence as a railroad brakeman's ghost, destined to remain forever at the sight of his untimely death. He continually waves his signal lantern as a warning to all who come to visit."

Still, other legends have developed concerning the lights. Some say it is the ghost of an Indian dancing on the power lines. Other locals attest to the fact that the lights start over Lake Superior and make their way inland.

The Paulding lights persist; eyewitnesses claim to have seen the lights way back at the turn of the century, while on their way to the train depot in Watersmeet.

Peculiar Ancient Tablets

In the late 1800's and early 1900's ancient tablets were unearthed throughout Michigan that were engraved with strange hieroglyphics and pictographs.

Records indicate that a priest, named James Savage from Detroit, ventured northward to excavate relics and unearthed 22,000 artifacts. When Savage died, he left all the artifacts with Notre Dame University.

The hieroglyphics on the tablets he discovered are similar to those found on relics in Egypt, Greece and France. According to archaeological researchers, some of the writing resembles ancient Hebrew writing and appears to give reference to Biblical history. Archaeological researcher Lois Benedict, said "A few of the tablets depict the battle between a good and evil angel, the event of creation, a universal flood and what is thought to be a depiction of the tower of Babel."

The many relics found throughout Michigan are not without controversy. There are questions concerning the authenticity of the artifacts. According to Benedict, professors from several universities studied the relics and concluded that people hoping to cash in on money created fake relics and planted them. As far as she knows, the tablets have never been carbon dated; however, her conclusion is that there is a mixture of genuine and fake tablets.

Pictured Rocks

The shoreline of Lake Superior displays images and forms that are so extraordinary; it is as though the hand of a colossal artist sculpted the breath-taking monument. Because of this natural splendor, in 1966, the United States established "The Pictured Rocks". The forty-mile stretch of rock cliffs, along the coastline from Munising to Grand Marais was the very first national lakeshore.

The Cambrian Sandstone cliffs rise out of the crystal blue waters some two-hundred feet in places. The wind and waves have carved the rocks into pillars, arches, caves and other fascinating forms. Oxides of copper, manganese, iron, and organic minerals add varying hues and depth to the magnificent natural sculptures. Some of the rocks have such artistic shapes that they have been given names such as Miner's Castle, Indian Head and Battleship's Row.

The images are most prominent along the fifteen miles of shoreline between Sand Point and Little Beaver Lake. Boat tours are available for the best view of Pictured Rocks. A walking trail also exists for the less seafaring.

Many Native Americans believed that there were spirits in the rocks and trees. What did the "Indian Head" and other images represent in their ancient lore?

Primitive Pyramids

There are theories that an anonymous group of people existed in Michigan who built pyramid type structures. Scientists from the University of Wisconsin and Michigan Tech. have studied two pyramid-shaped formations in Ontonagon. The height of one is fifty-six feet while the other is sixty-seven feet.

There are a number of theories as to who actually built these structures. Some say it was the Addenda or Hopewell Indians. If this were the case, why would they build pyramid type structures, rather than the usual rounded-top mounds?

Others theorize that they were the work of Egyptian miners who came to the Upper Peninsula to mine copper. They speculate that the pyramids were markers left by these people to indicate to other travelers that they had been there.

More conjectures state that refugees from the lost continent of Atlantis escaped to Michigan and left these markers to let other survivors know that Atlanteans had made it through the major catastrophe of their continent. There are numerous theories; however, the bottom line is, the mystery of these remarkable configurations prevails.

Raining Fish

One of the most unusual and spectacular things that has happened in Michigan occurred on the Great Lakes in 1986. According to the book, *Forces of Nature, by Time- Life,* there are records that indicate fish have rained down from the skies over Lake Michigan.

As unlikely as this may sound to some, the phenomenon exist. There have been reports of fish-falls from the earliest times. Some of these accounts go as far back as ancient Egypt.

During a heavy storm in 1986, smelt bombarded a fishing trawler sailing on Lake Michigan. The three-man crew was busy fighting high waves and engine failure when loads of smelt began raining down on their vessel. The fish fell in such abundant numbers that the trawler nearly capsized.

This may sound incredible to some; however, one meteorologist from Northwestern Michigan College says that this type of spectacle is not impossible. Gale force winds as well as waterspouts often contribute to such occurrences. High winds pick some of these lighter fish right up out of the water.

Reports from other parts of the world include falls of fish, frogs, snakes, beetles and ants. Fishing in Michigan may be easier than you thought!

Sanilac Petroglyphs

An immense forest fire swept through the Lower Peninsula in 1881, burning away brush and grass along the banks of the Cass River. The devastation revealed the only ancient petroglyphs ever discovered in Michigan. The prehistoric drawings, engraved into the aggregate, express relevant symbols of an ancient Indian culture.

The fire exposed more than one-hundred ancient carvings of birds, animals, tracks, spirals, crosses and waves. The most notable depiction, deeply carved into a sandstone outcrop, is of a warrior with his feet apart and his bow drawn.

Dating back to the Late Woodland Period, Native Americans created these remarkable, ancient illustrations 300 to 1,000 years ago. The specific purpose of the carvings is yet unknown.

The Sanilac Petroglyphs historic site, near Cass, Michigan, is a 238-acre park where the images can be viewed. A pavilion protects the most expressive of the designs. From the petroglyphs, a 1.5-mile trail winds through the 238-acre state park unit.

Sea Monsters of the Great Lakes

Does Nessie, Scotland's fabled Loch Ness Monster have a cousin? Tales of strange "monsters" in Lake Michigan have come down from ancient times.

The Native Americans of Michigan believed in a sea monster called, "Mishi-peshu (Mish-ee-pee-shew). They referred to it as the "great panther" that lived beneath the lakes and alleged this monster preyed on the flesh of lake travelers. They thought that the thrashing of the creature's enormous tail created the waves in the Great Lakes. Before they journeyed over the waters of the big lakes, they would offer a sacrifice to appease the terrifying spirit.

Scientists all over the world, continue to find species in the oceans, considered extinct for thousands of years. Is it possible that strange creatures still exist in the Great Lakes, unknown to man?

In 1985 and 1987, there were reports of sightings of a huge serpent-like creature in Lake Erie. Rangers at East Harbor State Park have reports from several eyewitnesses on at least three separate occasions. At one time, a five-thousand dollar reward was offered to anyone who could capture such a creature alive. Lake Erie covers an area of 240 miles, ten times the size of Loch Ness, therefore; capturing such a creature would be much more difficult than capturing one in Scotland's Loch Ness.

Sinking City

There are large portions of land that have literally caved in underneath the feet of those living in the town of Negaunee, a small community east of Ishpeming in the Upper Peninsula. Whole streets are abandoned due to cave-ins, leaving certain areas of Negaunee to resemble a ghost town.

Entire blocks are sealed off and hundreds of homes, churches and other buildings have been moved across town. One of the most bizarre things that occurred in Negaunee involves the town's cemetery. The entire cemetery was dug up, removed, and taken to another location, when the cemetery started caving in and several caskets fell into old mine shafts.

One family in Negaunee woke up one morning to discover that their front yard had caved in. In another area, where a huge cave-in occurred, the road abruptly ends and becomes a huge pit. A similar incident happened in Iron Mountain, when a section of highway ruptured and several cars fell into the chasm.

According to historian and researcher, Fred Rydholm of Marquette, there are nearly 180 miles of abandoned mines underneath the adjoining towns of Negaunee and Ishpeming. Some of the extensive mines beneath the town have collapsed, causing the ground above to give way.

Spirit Island

Historically, Native Americans of Michigan believed that sacred islands where the dwelling-places of spirits. They attached great importance to the resident "manitous", or spirits. The North and South Manitou Islands are the namesakes of these spirits.

When approaching the Manitou Islands by boat, people often see mirages that distort the shape and size of the islands. The mists, vapors, and bending light rays make the islands seemingly strange. Those approaching the harbors will perceive the islands as incredible and ever changing shapes.

Sailors have reported that upon approaching, the islands suddenly vanish from sight. Moments later, they may see something that looks like a large arm reaching off the island and extending up over the surface of the water. At other times, objects that looked like castles would appear, with walls and towers, and huge piles of ruins. Unexpectedly, all of these would vanish and then just as swiftly, new forms would appear.

The Indians attributed these odd and ever-changing perceptions of the islands, to the all-powerful spirits, or "manitous". They would go there to perform their mysterious rites to pacify the manitous.

St. Elmo's Fire

In maritime lore, seafaring mariners believed in supernatural manifestations. Sailors of the Great Lakes would sometimes see the masts of their ships come alive with a flickering blue light referred to as St. Elmo's fire.

Many ancient sailors believed that St. Elmo watched over them and kept them safe from storms and sea monsters. When the blue light would appear atop the mast, mariners thought it was St. Elmo bravely guiding his people to a safe harbor.

The Encyclopedia Britannica states the name St. Elmo is an Italian corruption, through Saint' Elmo, of St. Erasmus, the patron saint of Mediterranean sailors who regarded St. Elmo's fire as the visible sign of his guardianship.

According to meteorologists, St. Elmo's fire is actually an unusual weather phenomenon produced by an electrical static discharge. When there is a lot of electricity in the air, such as during a thunderstorm, objects that point upward can take on an electrical charge and emit the blue or greenish glow. This phenomenon occurs in Michigan from time to time. It usually appears as a tip of light on the very tops of pointed objects such as church towers and the masts of ships. St. Elmo's fire is often accompanied by crackling or fizzing noises.

Strange Shakings

In the early 1990's, residents of Ahmeek and three other small towns in the Upper Peninsula were awakened by strange tremors. Michigan is not accustomed to earthquakes. However, what makes the tremors so unusual is that they could not be confirmed as earthquakes. Scientists who investigated these shakings could not figure out if they were sonic booms, freezing ground or some type of mine collapse. Whatever the cause, it was never determined.

One of the last reports on this subject stated that an associate professor of mining engineering at Michigan Tech. was going to look into the bizarre shakings. The professor's theory was that during mining days, a large amount of rock was removed from the mines. He speculates that pillars supporting an abandoned mine collapsed and caused tons of rock to fall. A huge collapse could have very easily shaken the ground.

This was just one of the theories of what happened. In due time, this situation is likely to happen again. The unusual rumblings in Michigan's Upper Peninsula remain a mystery to many.

Surprising Sinkholes

Many people are familiar with the large sinkholes in Florida that show up without warning and devour homes and property. However, most are not aware of the fact that northern Michigan has quite a few of these abyss sites.

The strange devouring pits are in a number of counties in northern Michigan. An abyss in Montmorency County measures one-quarter mile across from rim to rim. There are also sinkholes in Presque' Isle County. "Drift sinks", that have thick soils over them, are in Cheboygan, Otsego and Montmorency Counties.

Some of Michigan's sinkholes are huge. There is a 29-acre preserve west of Alpena called the Steven's Twin Sinks Preserve, Karst Conservancy, where the public can view three sinkhole sites. A 2.4-mile interpretive trail takes you past five depressions, some more than 100 feet deep. The largest sinkhole there is 220 feet in diameter and 83 feet deep.

Sinkholes have unusual characteristics. The bottom of the chasm can be as much as twenty degrees cooler than at the rim. In addition, plants grow in the sinkholes that do not grow locally, rather two-hundred miles north of Michigan. Various wood ferns growing together at the bottom have been known to hybridize and form rare species.

Tornados of Fire

One of the weirdest catastrophes ever recorded in Michigan is the report of a pair of unusual firestorms that sent flaming whirlwinds through several Michigan and Wisconsin towns on October 8, 1871. That summer a drought lasted from July 8 all the way through October. Loggers and sawmill operators had been battling small forest fires for weeks.

Intense fires can create massive updrafts and hurricane winds. These winds generate powerful vortexes, or fiery tornados. The tornados of fire devastated 23 towns and villages. An estimated 1,500 people perished, and 1.3 million acres of timberland burnt. Survivors of the Michigan blaze described seeing a great black, balloon-shaped object whirling over the tops of trees.

Reporters of the day claimed that houses exploded in to flames and that the atmosphere itself was nearly burning. People died just breathing in the air. People's clothing and hair burst into flames. Children were lowered into wells, but perished anyway because merchants had put their goods in the well earlier in hopes of preserving them.

On this same night, the great Chicago fire was kindled. The Michigan-Wisconsin firestorm killed five times as many people on the same day.

Treasure Troves

Many people are surprised to discover that Northern Michigan is the secret home of buried treasure. The discovery of gold, silver, copper, diamonds and other precious stones has taken place for centuries.

Michigan had a gold rush in the late 1800's, when the first mine was opened, that lasted until 1897. The Chicago and Northwest Railroad built a railway specifically related to mining gold in Michigan. There were as many as nine gold mines open at one time in the Upper Peninsula. The Rope Mine was opened as late as 1989.

Gold has been discovered in over one-hundred places and in just about every river system or gravel pit in Michigan. The best gold deposits in Michigan are in the western Upper Peninsula, from Iron Mountain to Marquette.

Some believe that the Upper Peninsula contains the largest diamond field in North America because of the kimberlitic pipes in the region. At least four major corporations, as well as representatives from Africa, have searched for diamonds in Michigan.

The mining of copper in Michigan dates back thousands of years. Tons of copper has been mined in the Keweenaw Peninsula since the 1860's and helped power America's electrical industry.

Underwater Passages

Higgins Lake, located near Houghton Lake, has presented an enigma for Michiganders. For years, anglers have wondered why certain species of lake trout usually found only in the Great Lakes are now in Higgins Lake. These fish are not in any other inland lake in Michigan. In examining this situation, researchers have theorized that underwater passageways from Lake Michigan are feeding the inland lakes.

Tales about the lake having underwater passageways have prevailed since the late 1800's. Historians claim that around the turn of the century a man drowned in Higgins Lake. After weeks of searching, his corpse reportedly surfaced in Lake Huron. This seemed to indicate the presence of underground channels connecting the Great Lakes to the inland lakes.

There may be a number of connecting passageways from the Great Lakes to inland lakes, as well as some inland lakes to other inland lakes. Some researchers have gone so far as to speculate that there are certain areas in the channels big enough to allow the passage of a small boat. A Native American legend says that Michigan's sea monster Mishi-Peshu traveled these waterways.

Unexpected Prehistoric Creatures

Archeologist and geologists, along with some average Michiganders have discovered the fossilized remains of some strange and unexpected prehistoric creatures. Mammoths and mastodons, saber toothed tigers and prehistoric camels roamed the lands of ancient Michigan. Whales and walruses, giant beavers, armored fishes and even sharks swam the water systems of the Great Lakes regions.

Margaret Anne Skeels' report, *The Mastodons and Mammoths of Michigan*, stated that as of 1962, 163 American mastodon fossils had been unearthed in Michigan. Most remains were found in bogs. In prehistoric times, Michigan was covered with mucky bogs; and once the elephant-like creatures sunk into the muck they were instantly buried.

Walruses, whales and sharks most likely ventured into the Great Lakes when the rivers flowing to the Atlantic Ocean were extremely high and deep. These species could probably not be sustained in the Great Lakes because there was not the proper food for their diet.

Rock quarries and Low lakes and ponds are the best places to search for vertebrate fossils. You might find the remains of prehistoric fishes.

Vanishing Villages

There are about 275,000 acres of sand dunes in Michigan. These magnificent areas are unique and fragile environments that provide countless benefits to Michigan, its residence and ecology.

Like living things, the dunes move from one place to another. They have swallowed trees, farms and entire towns like Newburyport; founded along the sandy hills of Lake Michigan. The dunes at Silver Lake are eating up a neighborhood. Some creep along, moving only a few inches annually. However, the dunes near Benton Harbor are recorded to have moved 22 feet in a two-year period.

The only trace of Singapore, Michigan is an occasional wall or chimney that can be seen with the shifting dunes. The thriving lumbering town, established near the mouth of the Kalamazoo River, fought a losing battle with the sand until 1875. A plaque, in nearby Saugatuck, declares: "Beneath the sands near the mouth of the Kalamazoo River lies the site of Singapore..."

Land developers from New York and Philadelphia came to Michigan in the mid 1800's and founded the town of Port Sheldon along a channel, north of the present city of Holland. A hotel and sawmill were constructed for the growing town. When the sand began filling in the channel, they attempted to dredge it out with no success. Within a year, they gave up the town and returned east.

Vikings in Michigan

Some archaeologists and historians believe there is evidence that Viking explorers came to Michigan. According to the book, *Viking Mettles, by Johan G.R. Baner, (a Viking and Native American scholar)* early in the 11th century a band of Vikings, led by Vidor Viking, penetrated the Upper Peninsula and operated copper mines on Isle Roy ale.

Baner bases his theory on a runic inscription found in the province of Helsingland, Sweden. The inscription tells of Vidor's voyage to a place called "Bigmouth", near Vineland, the Viking name for America. According to Baner's report, the writing goes on to tell how the Vikings made a journey up many rivers to a huge fresh-water sea and went to a big island to mine copper. Baner says that this island was Isle Roy ale.

Baner says there is other evidence that the Vikings visited the Great Lakes region. Scientists confirm a genuine runic inscription and an ancient weapon, found in Minnesota.

There are Native American legends that tell of white men who wore armor and helmets, with eagle's wings on them. The legends say these men came to Michigan to mine copper. There are also Native Americans whose ancestors spoke Swedish, the native tongue of Vikings.

Volcanoes in Michigan

Geologists say that northern Michigan was once a region filled with volcanic activity. Those living in northern Michigan and the Upper Peninsula are living right near the mid-continental volcanic rift.

The rift zone extends north of Michigan and toward the Keweenaw Peninsula. The rift system has three arms, one of which goes right down through northern Lower Michigan. Geophysical surveys, including gravity and magnetic data confirm this fact.

Theories state that an ancient volcano was located in Lake Superior. The kimberlitic pipes found there are indicative of volcanic activity. Copper is a by-product of volcanoes and the Keweenaw Peninsula is renowned for its copper reserves, adding further proof that volcanoes existed in Michigan.

Geologists say that although volcanic activity in Michigan is unlikely to occur in the future, the possibility is not completely out of the question.

Water Running Uphill

There are several gravity-defying areas in Michigan. One of them is located on a stretch of road in Benzie County. This area, mentioned earlier in this book, is the place where cars and other objects appear to roll uphill.

Another area is unique in somewhat the same way. However, at this location in Missaukee County, an even stranger occurrence appears to be happening. This phenomenon involves a ditch that runs along an upward inclining stretch of road.

When the snow melts in the spring, or after a heavy rainfall, the water in this ditch will seem to be running uphill. On the road beside the ditch, a car placed in neutral will not roll uphill. The result is that there is something very bizarre happening when the water in the ditch right next to the road will seem to run uphill, but objects on the road right next to it will not.

Ancient people believed in an earth force called the "dragon force", a natural magnetic force of the earth. They believed underground rivers and channels of water followed this force. Another peculiar aspect of this site is that it is located only one mile from the mysterious Missaukee mounds and natural springs are near by.

Waterfalls & Fountains

Those who travel in Michigan will have an excellent opportunity to enjoy the soothing effects of water. For centuries, man has been fascinated with the hypnotic flow of fountains and waterfalls. Some historical cultures even considered water divine.

Michigan finds its home among the largest fresh water supply in the world and in so many ways that water puts on a beautiful exhibit. It is said that you cannot go anywhere in Michigan without being within five miles from some sort of water system. Be it one of the many creeks, streams, rivers, ponds, lakes or GREAT Lakes. The water that surrounds us puts Michigan on display even from space, distinguishing our place on the landmasses of the world.

There are approximately 150 waterfalls in Michigan and 148 of them are in the Upper Peninsula. The most renowned is Tahquamenon Falls. In the Lower Peninsula, one is located off the Manistee River near Mesick and the other, the Ocqueoc Falls, is near Rogers City.

Michigan is also the home of the largest water fountain in the world. The city of Grand Haven constructed a fountain the length of a football field in 1963. Colored lights beam on streams of water while music plays to create the world's largest, musical, water fountain.

Waterspouts

Since primitive times strange and eerie waterspouts have appeared over the Great Lakes. These dark and sinister funnels are literally a tornado of water that appears at the end of the summer season, when the water temperature is near the highest level of the year. Waterspouts are most likely to occur when the air is cold and moist, and wind speeds are relatively light.

There are two types of waterspouts. Tornadic waterspouts are typical land tornados that travel out over the water. They are usually coupled with thunderstorms and can be very large, capable of significant damage.

Fair weather waterspouts occur more frequently than the tornadic variety. They form exclusively over open water. When the water temperature is warm and humidity is the lowest, they develop on the surface of the water and ascend skyward. They are usually small and less dangerous; lasting from two to twenty minutes, and travel at speeds of 10 to 15 knots.

Mike Jacobson, a meteorology professor at Northwestern Michigan College, says there are as many as six waterspouts on the Great Lakes a year. He believes that many waterspouts go undetected and that several more may occur than are recorded each year.

For More Information

ANCIENT STATUES *Fred Rydholm*   906-249-3814
BIGFOOT Contact *Art Kapa*   517-843-6302
CAVES
THE CURIOUS CANAL Cadillac, MI   800-22-Lakes
DOLMEN ALTARS *Fred Rydholm*   906-249-3814
FLOATING ISLAND Interlochen, MI   231-276-7141
GRAVITY HILL Benzonia, MI   231-882-5801
GREAT LAKES TRIANGLE Grand Island Shipwreck Tours   906-387-4477
GREEN SUNSETS
HISTORICAL INDIAN HIGHWAYS   800-22-LAKES
LARGEST LIVING ORGANISM Crystal Falls, MI   800-255-3620
LOST GEOMETRICAL GARDENS Contact U of M Museum
METEORITES Contact U of M astronomy Dept.
MICHIGAN'S STONEHENGE Beaver Island, MI   231-547-2101
MISSAUKEE MOUNDS Lake City, MI   231-839-4969
THE PAULDING LIGHTS Paulding, MI   906-852-3500
PECULIAR ANCIENT TABLETS *Fred Rydholm*   906-249-3814
PICTURED ROCKS Munising, MI   906-387-2379
PRIMITIVE PYRAMIDS Ontonagon, MI   Write to: *Ancient American Magazine*
            3200 W. 205 St.
            Olympia Fields, IL 69461
SANILAC PETROGLYPHS Cass, MI   517-872-3434
SINKING CITY Negaunee, MI
SPIRIT ISLAND Manitou Ferry Serv.   231-256-9061
SURPRISING SINKHOLES Alpena, MI   517-356-2202
TREASURE TROVES Ishpeming, MI   906-486-4841
UNDERWATER PASSAGES Houghton Lake, MI   800-248-LAKE
VANISHING VILLAGES Silver Lake, MI   616-873-2247
VIKINGS IN MICHIGAN See *"Viking Mettles"* by Johan G.R. Baner
WATERFALLS & FOUNTAINS Grand Haven, MI   616-842-0529

If you have an unusual
fact or phenomenon
about the great state of Michigan
or about an odd Michigander
and would like to see your story
in a future edition of
"*MYSTIC MICHIGAN*",
please send your information to:

Mark Jager
Zosma Publications
P.O. Box 24
Hersey, Michigan 49639

or via email
zosmabooks@gmail.com

ORDER FORM
The following items are available by
Mark Jager

Qty.	Item	Total
	Mystic Michigan #1... $7.95	
	Mystic Michigan #2... $7.95	
	Mystic Michigan #3... $7.95	
	Mystic Michigan #4... $7.95	
	Mystic Michigan #5... $7.95	
	Mystic Michigan #6... $7.95	
	Mystic Michigan #7... $7.95	
	Mystic Michigander... $7.95	
	Mystic Michigan #1 Audio Book ... $12.95	
	Tripping America The Fantastic ... $7.95	
	SUBTOTAL	
	SHIPPING	
	SALES TAX 6%	
	TOTAL	

SHIPPING CHARGES
Please send $2.00 for shipping & handling for the first item purchased. Add $1.00 for each additional item.

THANK YOU!

Name_____

Street_____

City_____State_____Zip_____

Send order with check or money order to:

Zosma Publications
PO Box 24
Hersey, MI 49639

Orders ship USPS
Allow 1 week for delivery

Notes

Notes